T0363790

CATS

CATS

JULIANNA PHOTOPOULOS

This pocket edition first published in 2023

First published in a hardback edition in 2022

Copyright © 2023 Amber Books Ltd

All rights reserved. No part of this publication may be reproduced, stored in a retrieval system, or transmitted in any form or by any means, electronic, mechanical, photocopying, recording, or otherwise, without prior written permission of the copyright holder.

Published by
Amber Books Ltd
United House
London N7 9DP
United Kingdom
www.amberbooks.co.uk
Instagram: amberbooksltd
Pinterest: amberbooksltd
Twitter: @amberbooks

ISBN: 978-1-83886-257-2

Project Editor: Michael Spilling
Designer: Keren Harragan
Picture Research: Terry Forshaw

Printed in China

Contents

Introduction 6

Wild Cats 8

Shorthair Cats 42

Longhair Cats 102

Cat Behaviour 148

Kittens 188

Picture Credits 224

Introduction

Cats don't really have nine lives. But cats are exceptional at climbing trees, jumping from high places and always landing on their paws. Cats can also stalk and pounce on prey such as rats, mice and snakes, and keep both our houses and gardens free from them. These natural hunters still possess many instincts and behaviours from their wild predator ancestor, the African wildcat (*Felis lybica*). Despite their inner wild, our furry friends make great companions – as a matter of fact, they

developed meowing to exclusively communicate with us! All cats – both domestic and wild – belong to the family called Felidae. Cats were first domesticated in the Near East around 7500 BCE because it suited them to live close to human settlements. The development of cat breeds started in the mid-19th century when like-minded cat owners began to form clubs and put on shows and competitions. Now broadly divided into shorthairs and longhairs, there are an estimated 700 million house cats worldwide and, no matter their breed, all members are of one species: *Felis catus*.

ABOVE:
One of the most popular breeds around the world is the modern Persian with a flat face and a long, silky coat.

OPPOSITE:
This adorable Russian blue kitten is known for its beautiful short, dense silver-blue coat.

Wild Cats

Wild cats are famous for their imposing appearance and hunting skills. Most of them – like the ocelot or the tiniest rusty-spotted cat – are small. But others, such as the lion and tiger, are big. In total, there are 41 species of cats in the world – including the domestic cat. These can generally be found alone, roaming wild in a range of habitats, from tropical rainforests to deserts and mountains, across Europe, Africa, Asia and North and South America.

Each species has distinct strategies to survive and distinctive coat colours and patterns that allow them to blend in with their environment. In the wild, cats are most active at dawn and dusk, which coincides with the most opportune times for hunting their prey.

Cats belong to the Felidae family and are divided into two main sub-groups: the Pantherinae, or big cats, and the smaller Felinae. Bigs cats – the lion, tiger, leopard, snow leopard, clouded leopard and jaguar – are distinguished for their roar, whereas the smaller cats can only purr. But to make things more confusing, not all big cats can roar. Smaller cats, which includes the domestic cat, are broken down into seven groups, or lineages. Sadly, most wild cats are now either endangered or threatened, mainly due to habitat loss and poaching.

OPPOSITE:

Large predator
The Eurasian lynx is the third largest predator in Europe after the brown bear and the wolf. However, it is a medium-sized wild cat and belongs to the smaller cat sub-group called Felinae.

Eurasian lynx
As its common name suggests, the species *Lynx lynx* is found throughout most of Eurasia. Its black-spotted winter coat can vary from silver-grey to greyish brown, while it is more reddish or brown in the summer. With black ear tufts and a short tail, it is the largest of the four members of the *Lynx* genus.

OPPOSITE:
Canada lynx
This North American species, *Lynx canadensis*, lives in forested areas across Alaska, Canada and northern parts of the United States, largely coinciding with its main prey, the snowshoe hare. Its big rounded paws covered by thick fur allow it to walk and hunt in the snow. Despite its long legs, the lynx quietly waits and then pounces on its prey.

OPPOSITE & ABOVE TOP:
Bobcat
Also known as the red lynx, this North American species (*Lynx rufus*) takes its name from its "bobbed" tail. The bobcat is the smallest of the four members of the *Lynx* genus and is thought to have evolved from the Eurasian lynx, which crossed into America 2.6 million years ago.

ABOVE LOWER:
Iberian lynx
This endangered wild cat species, *Lynx pardinus*, is native to Spain and Portugal. Its coat is yellowish-red or tawny with dark brown or black spots. Of all the *Lynx* members, the Iberian lynx is the most densely spotted. Males eat one rabbit a day, while females with kittens feed on three!

OPPOSITE:
Andean mountain cat
The endangered species *Leopardus jacobita* is native to the high Andes mountains of South America. It has an ashy-grey coat with black or brown spots and stripes, and a long, bushy tail, banded with dark rings.

LEFT TOP:
Geoffroy's cat
This South American species, *Leopardus geoffroyi*, is named after French naturalist Étienne Geoffroy Saint-Hilaire. Its coat varies from tawny to grey and has many small black spots. It is about the size of a house cat, but it has a more flattened head and a shorter tail.

LEFT BELOW:
Margay
A skilful climber of Central and South America, the small wild cat species *Leopardus wiedii* is also known as the tree ocelot. It looks similar to the ocelot – having brown fur marked with dark brown or black spots and streaks – but is smaller, with a longer tail.

ABOVE:

Oncilla

Also known as the northern tiger cat, this small spotted cat often overlaps with its close relatives, the ocelot and margay, in Central and South America. However, this species (*Leopardus tigrinus*) is smaller and has a narrower muzzle. It is one of the smallest South American wild cats, only weighing 1.5–3 kg (3.3–6.6 lb).

LEFT:

Agile acrobat

A margay, or tree ocelot, rests on a tree in a Costa Rican forest. Margays spend most of their time on trees, resting during the day and hunting rodents, monkeys, birds and insects at night. Like a skilful acrobat, these wild cats can grasp branches with both front and back paws, ricochet off a surface in mid-leap, jump up 2.4 m (8 ft) and 3.7 m (12 ft) horizontally, and climb down headfirst.

LEFT:
What's that sound?
A red jaguarundi
(*Herpailurus
yagouaroundi*) found
in Central and South
America snarls and
hisses. Jaguarandis can
be grey or red and are
very vocal, using at least
13 different sounds to
communicate – from
purring, whistling,
yapping and chattering to
chirping like a bird. They
are closely related to the
cheetah and puma.

ABOVE:
Cheetah
This large spotted
cat species (*Acinonyx
jubatus*), with a small
rounded head, short
snout and black tear-like
face marks, is native to
Africa and central Iran.
The newborn cubs have
a thick yellowish-grey
coat on their backs
called a "mantle", which
is thought to act as
camouflage. Cheetahs
live in three main social
groups: females with
their cubs, males and
solitary males.

OPPOSITE TOP:

Champion sprinter
Cheetahs are the fastest animals on land, accelerating to more than 96.6 km/h (60 mph) in three seconds from standing still. Besides being slender and very muscular, cheetahs have a long flexible spine and a large heart, lungs and nostrils that help with their speed, which can reach up to 120.7 km/h (75 mph). They hunt mostly during the day by closely stalking their prey and then burst into speed.

RIGHT & OPPOSITE BOTTOM:

Ambush predator
Native to the Americas, the solitary mountain lion (*Puma concolor*) is the largest native American cat. Though large like a big cat, it belongs to the smaller cat subfamily called Felinae. It is known by many names, including cougar, puma and panther. It sits and waits for its prey – mostly deer and other mammals – before jumping on to their backs. Thanks to their large paws and long back legs, mountain lions can leap up to 5.5 m (18 ft) high into a tree.

RIGHT TOP:
African golden cat
Caracal aurata is native
to the rain forests of
West and Central Africa.
Its coat colour varies
from chestnut to grey or
black, usually with spots.
Twice the size of a house
cat, the African golden
cat resembles its close
relatives – the caracal
and the serval – but it
has small, rounded ears
without tufts.

RIGHT BOTTOM:
Graceful leaper
A male serval (*Leptailurus
serval*) walks through the
grasses of its savannah
home in Africa. Servals
are medium-sized spotted
cats with large ears and
long legs. Active both
at night and in the day,
servals use their hearing
to locate their prey.

OPPOSITE:
Caracal
While its close relatives
– the African golden
cat and the serval – live
only in Africa, *Caracal
caracal* is found in both
Africa and western Asia.
Its name comes from the
Turkish *karrah-kulak*
meaning "cat with
black ears".

LEFT:

Asian golden cat

This medium-sized elusive species, *Catopuma temminckii*, is native to the north-eastern Indian subcontinent, South East Asia and China. Also known as Temminck's cat and Asiatic golden cat, it has many colours – from golden brown to reddish and buff-brown, or black.

ABOVE:

Marbled cat

The species *Pardofelis marmorata* lives in forests from the eastern Himalayan foothills to South East Asia. It is closely related to the Asian golden cat and bay cat, with all three making up the bay cat lineage.

LEFT:

Leopard cat

Not to be confused with the leopard, this small, spotted wild cat (Prionailurus bengalensis) is found in mainland Asia. Though about the same size as a house cat, the slenderer leopard cat has long legs and webbed paws. This wild cat was crossed with domestic cats in the 1970s and later gave rise to the Bengal.

OPPOSITE TOP:

Fishing cat
As its name suggests, this wild cat (*Prionailurus viverrinus*) mainly hunts fish. Living close to the water in South and South East Asia, fish make up about three-quarters of its diet. About twice the size of a house cat, the fishing cat can swim long distances – even underwater. This wild cat is the state animal of West Bengal.

LEFT:

Rusty-spotted cat
The rare species *Prionailurus rubiginosus* is the smallest wild cat -ck and flanks. It can be found in India, Sri Lanka and Nepal.

Pallas's cat

Named after the Prussian zoologist and botanist, Peter Simon Pallas, Pallas's cat is about the size of a house cat. Also known as *Otocolobus manul*, or manul, its long, thick grey fur keeps it warm and camouflaged in the rocky montane grasslands and shrublands of Asia and the Middle East.

European wildcat
Wildcats belong to
the *Felis* genus, which
includes the domestic
cat. This species is *Felis
silvestris*, or the European
wildcat, and could easily
be mistaken for a large
house cat. It is found in
parts of Europe, Turkey
and the Caucasus.

Asiatic wildcat
Also known as the Asian
steppe wildcat and Indian
desert cat, this African
wildcat subspecies, *Felis
lybica ornata*, spreads
from Central Asia to
north-east India.
It was a species of its own
until the 1940s.

African wildcat
This wildcat species, *Felis
lybica*, is the common
ancestor of our domestic
cats. Resembling tabbies,
it is estimated that the
African wildcat was
domesticated about 10,000
years ago in the Near
East. Until 2017, it was
considered the European
wildcat subspecies *Felis
silvestris lybica*.

Sand cat

This small, well-adapted desert wild cat is known as the sand cat, or *Felis margarita*. It has a sandy coat that provides incredible camouflage and its toes' long hairs protect its paws from the extremely hot and cold temperatures by forming an insulating cushion.

Black-footed cat

Weighing 1.1–2.45 kg (2.4–5.4 lb), the species *Felis nigripes* is the smallest wild cat in Africa. Its body is covered with black or brown spots and stripes, and only the soles of its paws live up to the common name black-footed cat.

Chinese steppe cat

The protected wild cat species *Felis bieti* is named after the 19th-century French missionary and naturalist Félix Biet. It is endemic to western China and is also known as the Chinese steppe cat, Chinese mountain cat and Chinese desert cat.

33

A wildcat litter
Though they resemble domestic tabbies, these Asiatic wildcats (*Felis lybica ornata*) are indeed wild. Compared to the house cat, Asiatic wildcats have longer legs.

RIGHT:

Jungle cat
Though the name suggests this wild cat is found in jungles, it is more common in densely vegetated wetlands, such as swamps, across the Middle East and Asia. Larger than a house cat, this species (*Felis chaus*) has an unspotted coat that varies from sandy to reddish-brown or grey.

OPPOSITE TOP:

Snow leopard
With pale green or grey eyes and exotically marked fur, this beautiful, elusive species, *Panthera uncia*, roams the mountain ranges of Central and South Asia. It is well adapted to the cold and the often snowy, rocky grounds and can easily chase its prey down steep mountainsides.

OPPOSITE BOTTOM:

Clouded leopard
Named after its distinctive cloud-shaped spots and stripes, the clouded leopard, or *Neofelis nebulosa*, is found from the foothills of the Himalayas across South East Asia to South China.

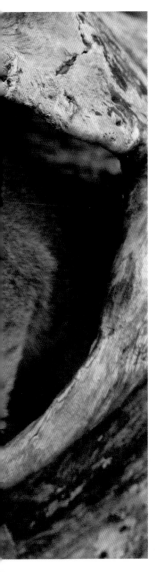

OPPOSITE:
Jaguar
The species *Panthera onca* is a member of the big cat subfamily Pantherinae. It is the only big cat found in the Americas, living across Central and South America, and weighs up to 96 kg (212 lb). Jaguars have a pale yellow to tawny coat covered with large spots called rosettes.

ABOVE:
Tiger
The endangered *Panthera tigris* is the largest living cat species. Its distinctive stripes help the tiger hide in forest habitats in parts of Asia. Tigers are solitary animals and have their own territories, which they mark with their scent. This charismatic species is the national animal of India, Bangladesh, Malaysia and South Korea.

ABOVE:
Tiger family
A tigress rests with her two cubs. This solitary species mates all year round and usually gives birth to two to three cubs. Tiger cubs stay with their mother for about two years, then leave to establish their own territories. Female cubs stay close to their mother's territory, while males travel farther away.

RIGHT:
Roar
An adult male lion with its prominent mane rests beside a lioness. This social species, *Panthera leo*, is native to Africa and India and spends most of its time resting, usually becoming active after dusk. Members of the *Panthera* genus, such as lions and tigers, roar rather than purr because of their enlarged larynx. A lion's roar can be heard up to 8 km (5 mi) away.

Shorthair Cats

Regardless of their shape and size, most cats have short hair. In fact, the first domesticated cats had short coats – just like their wild predator ancestors. Cats with short coats can move more freely, helping them be more efficient hunters.

Since the first domesticated cats, a large number of breeds have been developed with short coats. These often come in many colours and well-defined patterns, as well as their own distinctive features and personalities. In some cases, short hair has been taken to the extremes, like in the hairless breeds. Often as a result of a natural mutation, kittens would be born hairless or with a very fine fuzz-like coating. Through selection and careful breeding, new breeds such as the sphynx were created. Other unique coat features caused by genetic mutations are curly or wavy coats, as seen in rexed cats. Not all domestic shorthairs are of a particular breed. The majority of them – in fact, 95 per cent of house cats – are simply called "moggies" and have unknown or mixed progenitors.

Generally, shorthairs are easier to maintain because they require less grooming. However, each breed is unique and some still may shed more than others – especially when losing their seasonal thick undercoat.

OPPOSITE:
Oriental shorthair
With a long wedge-shaped head, almond-shaped eyes and large bat-like ears, this captivating chocolate-brown cat was developed in the 1950s by crossing the Siamese with domestic shorthairs. The first of the oriental shorthairs had rich dark brown coats and were known as Havanas. Now, the curious orientals come in many distinct colours and patterns.

Abyssinian
Also known as Abys, this charming and intelligent breed developed in the United Kingdom takes its name from Abyssinia – now Ethiopia – where it is believed to have originated. However, genetic research has found its ticked coat pattern – in which each hair has alternate bands of dark and light colours called "agouti" – may have stemmed from cats from coastal areas of north-eastern India.

OPPOSITE:
Wild look
With a deep reddish-brown and black ticked coat pattern, known as "usual", this original-coloured Abyssinian looks wild. In fact, ticked fur provides camouflage to many wild cats and other mammals. Other colours include blue and fawn with distinct ticking.

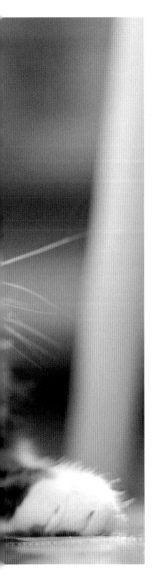

LEFT:
American shorthair
Formerly known as the domestic shorthair, this popular North American breed is believed to have descended from the first domestic cats brought to the United States from Europe by early pilgrims in the 1600s.

ABOVE:
American curl
With big eyes and unusual ears, this designer cat breed was originally long haired like its ancestor – a black female stray called Shulamith, discovered in California in 1981. Its curled ears are a result of a natural genetic mutation.

RIGHT TOP:

Asian

Also known as the Malayan, the friendly Asian was developed in the United Kingdom. Asian shorthairs come in four distinct varieties: Asian solid, Asian tabby, Asian smoke and the Burmilla. This sleeping Asian looks like it has a moustache.

RIGHT BOTTOM:

Arabian mau

Once a desert cat native to the Arabian Peninsula, this modern breed was developed in the 2000s to save its original features and qualities. Although the Arabian mau is very active and retains its hunting and territorial instincts, it is also loyal and makes a devoted house companion.

OPPOSITE:

American wirehair

Named after its rare springy, wiry coat, the American wirehair originated in Vernon, New York in 1966. The wiry coat – in which the hair tips are bent or twisted – is caused by a genetic mutation.

Desert lifestyle

The Arabian mau will eat almost anything, including animals, fruits and insects, because it originated in a harsh habitat where food was scarce. The natural breed can still be found in desert regions near human settlements. To avoid the summer heat, it usually sleeps during the day and becomes active around dawn and dusk.

Burmilla

This playful and yet easy-going breed gets its looks and personality from two cats: the Burmese and the chinchilla Persian. After an accidental mating in 1981, the Burmilla was born in the United Kingdom.

Bambino

A cross between the hairless sphynx and the short-legged munchkin, these unusual-looking cats got their name from the Italian word for "baby". Though they look naked, bambinos are usually covered with extremely fine hair. This experimental breed was created in 2005.

Australian mist

Taking nine years of development to become the first pedigree cat created in Australia, the Australian mist combines the breeder's favourite cats: Burmese, Abyssinian and domestic shorthairs.

Bengal
This exotically marked coat belongs to a very energetic and beautiful hybrid, created by crossing the wild Asian leopard cat with short-haired domestic cats like the Egyptian mau and the Abyssinian. It was previously known as the leopardette.

Burmese

As the name suggests, this cat originated in Burma. The first Burmese arrived in the United States in the 1930s from Burma, whereupon it was bred with the Siamese, creating the American Burmese. Burmese cats were later sent to the United Kingdom, where the breed got a distinct look with a longer head and body – the so-called European Burmese.

OPPOSITE RIGHT MIDDLE:
Brazilian shorthair
This attractive shorthair with expressive eyes is the first official breed from Brazil, as its name denotes. The Brazilian shorthair was developed using feral street cats that had originally been brought to the country by the Portuguese around 1500 CE.

OPPOSITE RIGHT BOTTOM:
Bombay
This attention-seeking black panther-like cat has distinctive black whiskers, nose, lips and fur and gold or copper eyes, all thanks to the sable Burmese and black American shorthair that make up its lineage.

ABOVE:
Chartreux
With a captivating thick blue-grey fur, the quiet Chartreux from France often appears to be "smiling". Though there are no records, legend has it that these cats were initially brought to France by Carthusian monks, makers of the Chartreuse liqueur.

British shorthair
This magnificent blue-grey cat with orange eyes, also known as the British blue, is one of the most ancient cat breeds. With many distinct colours and patterns, they were developed from British domestic cats – originally imported by the Romans – which interbred with local wildcats.

OPPOSITE:
Chausie
This breed was created in the 1990s by crossing domestic short-haired cats and the wild *Felix chaus* – from which its name is derived. The svelte Chausie has three coat colours and patterns: black, black grizzled tabby, and brown or brown-ticked tabby.

LEFT TOP:
Cats in Cyprus
These cats have been domesticated over time on the island of Cyprus. Also known as Cyprus or Cypriot cats, Saint Helen cats or Saint Nicholas cats, a standarized breed is being developed under the name Aphrodite giant or Aphrodite.

LEFT BELOW:
Colourpoint British shorthair
Often confused with the colourpoint shorthair because of its name, this stocky breed that shares a similar coat pattern with the Siamese was recognized in 1991. It has blue eyes and a typically large, rounded head with a short muzzle.

European shorthair
Resembling the original
domestic cats of Europe,
this calm and friendly
breed was developed
in Sweden. European
shorthairs can be kept
indoors and out, and
will clear both places of
rodents.

Cornish rex
This cat with a curly, or
"rexed", coat only has
one coat layer called
down hair or undercoat,
which is very fine. They
cannot tolerate the cold
and should be kept
indoors.

Devon rex
Similar to the Cornish
rex, this cat has a short
curly coat and whiskers
as a result of a mutation.
So, unlike its Cornish
cousin, it also has an
outer coat layer, called
guard hairs.

Donskoy

Also known as Don sphynx and Russian hairless, this wrinkled, hairless cat with large ears and almond-shaped eyes originated in Russia in the 1980s. Donskoy cats are descendants of a rescue kitten found in the streets of Rostov-on-Don. While some Donskoy cats are indeed hairless, others have partial fuzzy or wavy coats.

Japanese bobtail
As its name suggests, this
loyal cat from Japan has a
very short, or "bobbed",
curved tail. Traditionally
found in Japanese folklore
and art, it is said to bring
good luck.

Egyptian mau
This naturally spotted cat,
which originated in Egypt,
is said to be the fastest
house cat breed. Its spots
appear on the tips of its
hairs and its forehead is
typically marked with the
letter "M".

Lykoi
Resembling a werewolf
with its wiry look and thin
black and grey fur, this cat
is nicknamed "werewolf
cat" and "wolf cat".
In fact, lykoi cats get their
name from the Greek
word for "wolves".

Mekong bobtail
Legend has it that Mekong
bobtails were royal cats
and guardians of ancient
temples, which were gifted
to the Russian Emperor
Nicholas II in the
19th century.

LEFT:

German rex

This friendly breed from Germany has a short, curly coat and whiskers because of the same genetic mutation found in the Cornish rex. Despite the short coat, German rex cats still need to be regularly groomed and bathed.

ABOVE:

Highlander

Reaching up to 11 kg (25 lb), this heavyweight cat is a crossbreed of two experimental domestic cats, the desert lynx and the jungle curl. The rare Highlander cats are noted for their curled ears, tabby markings and short or bobbed tails.

ABOVE:
Kurilian bobtail
Named after the Kuril Islands in the North Pacific, this short-tailed breed is rare outside Russia and Japan. Its distinctive short, kinked tail is a natural mutation and ranges in length and formation from two to ten vertebrae.

OPPOSITE TOP:
Khao manee
This rare breed's name means "white jewel" in its native country Thailand. Also known as the diamond eye cat, the Khao manee is noted for its beautiful and diverse eyes, which can even be odd-coloured. Khao manees were previously kept and bred only by Thai royalty.

OPPOSITE BOTTOM:
Korat
With a silvery-blue coat, this ancient cat breed from Thailand is considered to bring good luck. The korat is known for its distinctive heart-shaped head and large green eyes. In fact, its eyes gradually change from amber in younger cats to green as they mature. It is one of the oldest breeds, thought to date to the 12th century.

RIGHT:

Ojos azules

Named in Spanish for its vibrant blue eyes, this very rare cat was discovered in the streets of New Mexico in 1984. They come in any coat length, colour or pattern but always have at least one deep-blue eye.

BELOW:

LaPerm

This hypoallergenic breed with long curly whiskers is named after its fleece-like wavy or curly coat. It first appeared on an American farm in the 1980s as a result of a natural genetic mutation.

OPPOSITE:

Manx

There are many tales about how the short-tailed or tailless cat of the Isle of Man, known as Manx, came to be. It is said that a tailless cat swam to the island after a shipwreck of the Spanish Armada, or the cat lost its tail on Noah's Ark. Some even say it is a mixture of a cat and a rabbit.

ABOVE TOP & BOTTOM:
Munchkin
Also known as the
"sausage", this curious
breed has legs that are
about half the average
length of other cats.
Despite its short legs
– caused by a natural
genetic mutation – the
munchkin can run and
sit on its back legs. Its
name is derived from
the fictional place
"Munchkin Country" in
the children's novel *The
Wonderful Wizard of Oz.*

RIGHT:
Moggy
Any short-haired house
cat of mixed or unknown
ancestry that does not
belong to a particular
breed is called a "moggy"
or "moggie". This tabby
short-haired cat has a
distinctive M-shaped
marking on its forehead.

ABOVE TOP & BOTTOM:

Peterbald

Crossed between the oriental shorthair and Donskoy, this graceful Russian breed can be born hairless, or have a very fine undercoat or a dense, stiff coat. However, those with a coat can lose it over time. Like other hairless breeds, the Peterbald is best kept indoors because its skin is sensitive to the cold and sunshine.

RIGHT:

Ocicat

Though resembling the ocelot, this spotted cat is nowadays a crossbreed of the Siamese, Abyssinian and American shorthair. Ocicats are often described as "dogs in a cat's body" because they can easily be trained.

Savannah
This spotted cat, with
huge ears and long legs,
looks a lot like the serval
– the native wild cat of
Africa known to be a
remarkable leaper.

Kanaani
With a long, slender
body and large tufted
ears, this spotted cat is a
crossbreed of short-
haired cats and the small
African wildcat. The
Kanaani was developed
in Israel in the 2000s and
takes its name from the
Biblical name "Canaan".

Oriental bicolour
With white always
covering its muzzle,
underside and legs,
this svelte short-haired
oriental bicolour was first
developed in the United
States. It comes in many
colours and patterns but
one-third of its body must
be white to be considered
a breed. Unlike the solid-
coloured oriental, which
typically has green eyes,
this cat's almond-shaped
eyes can be green, blue or
one of each.

ABOVE:

Russian white

As the name suggests, this breed has an entirely white coat. Russian whites were developed in a specific Australian breeding programme in 1971 by crossing short-haired cats from Siberia and the Russian blue.

RIGHT:

Pixiebob

Resembling the North American bobcat, this entirely domestic large cat has a thick brown-spotted tabby coat, tufted ears and a bobbed tail. Pixiebobs commonly have extra toes on their paws – a condition called polydactylism – which is only accepted in this breed standard.

Scottish fold

This breed with unusual folded ears was first discovered on a Scottish farm in the 1960s, giving it its name. Scottish fold kittens are born with straight ears, which usually start to fold within three weeks. Those cats that do not develop folded ears are called Scottish straights.

ALL:
Russian blue
With striking green eyes, the Russian blue's shiny,
dense coat comes in different shades of silver-blue. It is
thought to have originated in the port of Archangel in
Russia and was brought to northern Europe by sailors
in the 1860s.

Serengeti

This exotically spotted cat, inspired to resemble the wild African serval, stands out with its large ears and long legs and neck. Crossed between a Bengal and oriental shorthair in the mid-1990s, the Serengeti has a touch of the wild and loves climbing up to high spots.

Serrade petit

The rather newly discovered cat from France lives up to its name in that it is small. Nevertheless, it is very vocal and likes to be kept company and entertained. Reaching up to 4 kg (9 lb), the Serrade petit is not yet recognized as a breed by any cat registries.

Modern Siamese
The modern-style Siamese is a descendent of the native cats of Thailand – formerly known as Siam. When the original Siamese – now the Thai or wichien maat – became very popular in the United States and Europe, its features were taken to the extreme. Now, the modern Siamese has a very skinny body and an angular look.

Thai blue point
Not to be confused with the Thai or wichien maat, the Thai blue point is a korat cat from Thailand. However, the Governing Council of the Cat Fancy (GCCF) recognizes it separately. Instead of a blue coat, it has a colourpoint pattern seen in the Siamese.

Snowshoe
Named for its distinctive white paws, the snowshoe was first seen in kittens born to a Siamese cat in Philadelphia in the 1960s. The breed was developed by crossing the Siamese and American shorthair.

Selkirk rex

Unlike other curly-coated breeds, the cuddly Selkirk rex has a soft, luxuriant coat with erratic curls or waves. It typically has more curls around its neck and belly and its curly whiskers break off easily. Named after the Selkirk mountains, it originated in 1987 in Montana, United States.

Singapura

With a distinctive ticked coat and large eyes and ears, the often-mischievous Singapura is the smallest cat breed, weighing on average just 2–4 kg (4–9 lb). Singapuras take their name from Singapore, where they supposedly originated in the 1970s.

RIGHT & BELOW:
Sphynx
This cat that appears to be completely hairless has, in fact, a light covering of down on its wrinkled body, but it does lack whiskers. Named after the Egyptian sculpture of a mythical creature, the sphynx originated in Canada and is also known as the Canadian sphynx.

OPPOSITE:
Sokoke
Formerly known as the African shorthair, this rare breed with a ticked tabby pattern and long legs is native to the Arabuko Sokoke National Forest in Kenya. The Sokoke, or Sokoke forest cat, was developed from the feral cat called *khadzonzo*.

Suphalak

Often confused with the sable Burmese, this breed from Thailand has golden eyes and a reddish-brown copper coat throughout its body. Even its whiskers are brown, while its nose is a rosy-brown. The suphalak, along with the korat and wichien maat, appears in a book titled *The Cat Book Poems*, thought to date back to the Ayutthaya period (1351–1767).

Tonkinese

These very sociable and mischievous cats are a crossbreed of the Burmese and Siamese. Though the Tonkinese seems to be named after Tonkin – the northern region of Vietnam – the breed has no connection to the area.

Ukrainian levkoy
With inward-folding ears and little to no hair, this cat was developed in Ukraine using the unusual-eared Scottish fold and hairless Donskoy. Later, it was also crossed with oriental shorthairs and domestic cats. The Ukrainian levkoy is only recognized as a breed in Ukrainian and Russian cat fancier organizations.

Wichien maat
Also known as the Thai, this newly renamed breed is a descendent from the cats of old Siam. It is known as the wichien maat in Thailand, which translates as "diamond gold".

Toyger
This wild-looking cat was developed in the 1990s to resemble a "toy tiger" and raise awareness of tiger conservation. To get the tiger-marked coat, a striped short-haired cat was crossed with a Bengal.

Longhair Cats

Cats are also known for their soft, luxurious long coats. It is believed that the long hair in house cats – which can reach up to 12 cm (5 in) in length – was caused by a natural genetic mutation. Cats with fluffy coats first appeared in colder, isolated regions, most likely to deal with the harsh environment.

Longhairs were imported to Britain and France from Asia Minor, Persia and Russia in the late 16th century. Specifically, the ravishing Turkish Angoras are thought to be the original long-haired cats – though not as we know them today. Turkish Angoras were very popular until the 19th century, when people started preferring the Persians. Though Persians remain one of the favourites, other longhairs such as the semi-longhairs with a less fluffy undercoat are becoming increasingly popular. Like shorthairs, cats with an unknown ancestry – moggies – can also have long hair and commonly have features derived from a Persian. What's more, rare long-haired breeds with unusual ears or curly fur have been developed by crossing the shorthair version with longhair breeds.

Unlike shorthairs, cats with a fabulous long coat require more maintenance by their owners – some need to be brushed on a daily basis to prevent mats and tangles. Long hair usually goes hand in hand with more shedding, especially in warmer seasons. Be prepared to find hair on couches and carpets. The fur also picks up more dirt and detritus from outdoors, including leaves, twigs and even slugs!

OPPOSITE:
Maine coon
One of the most grandiose cats with a long coat is the North American native, Maine coon, nicknamed "the gentle giant".

Maine coon

Native to North America, the magnificent large Maine coon is named after New England's state Maine, where it first appeared. Exactly how it got there remains a mystery but it is believed to be closely related to the Norwegian forest cat and the Siberian. Its distinctive thick and waterproof coat, bushy tail and tufted ears allow the Maine coon to get through harsh winters.

American curl
This attractive rare breed originated in California as a long-haired stray with a black coat and unusual curled ears. As their name suggests, American curls' ears curl back at least 90 degrees, as a result of a natural mutation. Affectionate and alert, the American curl makes an excellent family companion.

OPPOSITE:

Oriental longhair

Formerly known as the British Angora, this breed was renamed in 2002 to avoid confusion with the Turkish Angora. With a long silky coat, oriental longhairs were developed in the United Kingdom in the 1970s in an effort to reproduce the Angora cat – a much-loved companion in the Victorian era.

LEFT TOP:

Birman

Also known as the "sacred cat of Burma", this striking colourpoint breed gets its name from the French *"Birmanie"* meaning "Burma". It is noted for its long silky fur, sapphire-blue eyes, Roman nose and white paws.

LEFT BOTTOM:

Point colouration

Like all colourpoint breeds, Birmans are born white and gradually begin developing their point markings after one to two weeks, and reach their full colour when they are two years old.

Balinese

With a silky coat and stunning sapphire-blue eyes, this long-haired version of the Siamese is highly sociable, inquisitive and often mischievous. Named after the graceful Balinese dancers, the Balinese was developed as a breed in the 1950s.

ABOVE:
Tail types
Similar to the Manx, Cymrics have distinct tail types
according to their length: the entirely tailless "rumpy";
a short knob of a tail or "rumpy-riser"; a "stumpy" ,
which is a curved or kinked tail; and the type with the
nearly normal-length tail, the "longy".

RIGHT:
British longhair
As the name suggests, this long-haired cat originated
in Great Britain. Except for its longer coat, it shares
the same features as its cousin, the British shorthair. In
fact, some registries do not consider the longhair to be
a separate breed. The British longhair is also known
as the Britannica in some parts of Europe and the
lowlander in the United States.

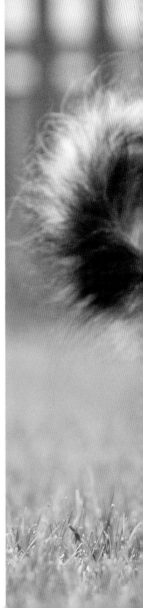

OPPOSITE TOP:
Highlander
Though resembling a wild bobcat with its long tabby coat, this cat is entirely domestic. Highlander longhairs have curled ears, a short, curled tail and distinctive facial features, such as a sloping forehead, blunt muzzle and noticeable whisker pads with long whiskers.

OPPOSITE BOTTOM:
Kurilian bobtail
As the name suggests, this short-tailed breed is native to the Kuril Islands in the North Pacific. Kurilian bobtails are rare and their tails are never the same – they have between two and ten vertebrae and curl in any direction.

LEFT ABOVE & BELOW:
Himalayan
Also known as the Himalayan Persian and colourpoint Persian, this cat with large blue eyes is a crossbreed of the Siamese and long-haired Persians. The Himalayan has round, cobby bodies with long, lush fur and short legs.

LEFT & ABOVE TOP:
Chantilly-Tiffany
Also known as the foreign longhair and Chantilly, this attractive breed originated in New York in the late 1960s with a long, chocolate-brown coat. It was once wrongly thought that the Chantilly-Tiffany was a long-haired Burmese. The Chantilly-Tiffany can have many coat colours, including black, and tabby patterns.

ABOVE BOTTOM:
Tiffanie
Often confused with the American Chantilly-Tiffany, this cuddly breed was developed in the 1980s in the United Kingdom as a long-haired version of the Asian shorthair. In fact, Tiffanies were an accidental result of the experimental breeding programme for the Asian cat called Burmilla.

Cyprus cats

Cats on the island of Cyprus have been breeding largely on their own for centuries. This has allowed them to develop into a distinct local cat variety that is on the way to being standardized under the name of Aphrodite giant.

Munchkin
This sociable short-legged cat is lively and loves playing with toys. Though its ability to jump is restricted by its short legs, caused by a random mutation, the munchkin can still climb and run.

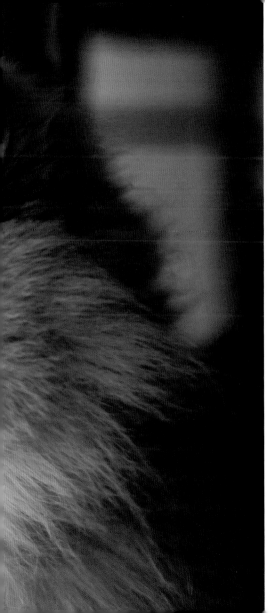

Minuet

Formerly known as the Napolean, this short, stunning cat is a crossbreed of a fluffy-coated Persian and a short-legged munchkin. Taking from both breeds, minuets are both gentle and active cats that like to spend time with their owners.

Nebelung

Also known as the longhaired Russian blue, this rare long-bodied breed with a soft, silver-tipped blue coat was developed in Colorado. Its name comes from the German word *Nebel* meaning "haze" or "mist", used to describe its shiny, long coat. The nebelung is a loving cat that adores sitting on laps and often shows its belly to receive affection from its owners.

ALL:
Norwegian forest cat
Very popular in Norway and Sweden, this natural
breed with its long, thick, waterproof coat is well
adapted to living in the harsh Scandinavian winters.
Its ancestors are believed to have been brought by the
Vikings, who used them on ships as a form of pest
control. The large and muscular Norwegian forest
cat – known as *skogkatt* in Norwegian – is a terrific
climber and hunter. It is the national cat of Norway.

Neva masquerade

The colourpoint version of the Siberian is this imposing cat with a very thick, long coat. Named after the Neva River in St Petersburg in Russia, the Neva masquerade is rare and some registries do not consider it to be a separate breed from the Siberian.

Scottish fold

This long-haired cat with small folded ears – which make its face look like that of an owl – is known by many names: Scottish fold, Highland fold, Scottish fold longhair, longhair fold and coupari. Scottish folds make great companions and can often be found snoozing on their backs and sitting with their legs stretched out and paws on their bellies.

Persian

With distinctive large rounded eyes, a flattened muzzle and long thick fur, this modern-type breed from Persia, or Iran, has been very popular since the 19th century. Persians, known to be gentle and affectionate, can have any coloured or patterned coat. Similar to the Siamese, there is an effort to preserve the older type, or the traditional Persian, which has a more pronounced muzzle.

Ragamuffin

Once a version of the ragdoll, this huge cat became a separate breed in 1994. Ragamuffins are noted for their dense, silky, rabbit-like fur and their friendly and docile personalities. Kittens are normally born white and gradually develop a colour pattern as they grow.

Selkirk rex
Named after the Selkirk
mountains, this cuddly
curly-coated breed loves
the attention. The Selkirk
rex was first discovered
in an American animal
rescue centre in Montana
and was later bred with
Persians to get these long,
loose curls.

ALL:
Ragdoll

These beautiful, easy-to-handle lap cats are one of the largest breeds. With big round blue eyes, a soft, thick coat and a long bushy tail, ragdolls supposedly get their name from the first litter of kittens becoming limp when picked up – like a ragdoll.

Turkish Van

Named after the Lake Van region of eastern Turkey, these large cats with a soft cashmere-like coat were first developed in the United Kingdom in the 1950s. Turkish Vans have a white coat with distinctive colour markings only on their heads and tails, which is known as the "Van pattern". A Turkish Van that is completely white and lacks markings is called a "Turkish Vankedisi".

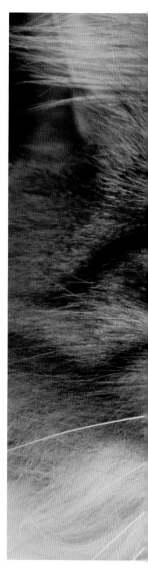

ALL:

Siberian forest cat

Also known as the
Siberian, this breed with
a thick, waterproof coat,
bushy tail and tufted
paw pads is the national
cat of Russia. Similar
to the Norwegian forest
cat, the strong and
muscular Siberian is well
adapted to harsh weather
conditions. It is also an
incredibly agile leaper.

OPPOSITE:
Somali
With a long, bushy tail, this is a descendent of the shorthaired Abyssinian, which sometimes produced kittens with long coats. At first, these were rejected by breeders, until others found them to be attractive – giving rise to the Somalis.

ABOVE:
York chocolate
This cat breed was named after its ancestor's dark chocolate-brown coat and the state of New York, where the breed was developed in 1983. The York chocolate, or York, is an excellent companion and comes in chocolate or lavender, as well as chocolate and white, and lavender and white.

Moggy

Long-haired house cats
that do not belong to
a distinct breed are
known as "moggies".
These could be of mixed
or unknown ancestry.
This long-haired cat
has a tabby coat, which
is distinguished by the
M-shaped marking on
its forehead.

Mixed breed

This orange cat of mixed
ancestry goes by many
names: domestic cat,
house cat, moggy or
moggie. In fact, these
mixed-breed cats are not
recognized as a breed at
all, but are still attractive.

Aphrodite giant

The Aphrodite giant or Aphrodite is a large, short-haired cat that is being developed as a standardized breed from Cyprus cats. The earliest records of these cats, dating back to 4 CE, describe how Saint Helena sent two boatloads of the cats from Egypt or Palestine to a Cypriot monastery infested with snakes.

Turkish Angora

This rare, fluffy, snow-white cat is native to the
Ankara region of Turkey, with records dating back
to around the 16th century. The Turkish Angora was
used to develop the Persian and disappeared as a breed
outside of Turkey until the 1960s. Although known for
their shimmering white coat and bushy tail, Turkish
Angoras come in many colours, shades and patterns.

Cat Behaviour

Cats often behave similarly to their wild ancestors, showing their inborn ability as predators. Though cats are active both day and night, they tend to be somewhat more active at night – their unique anatomy and senses are well adapted for hunting in low light. To conserve energy to stalk and pounce on their prey, cats spend most of their time sleeping. They also spend a lot of time grooming but enjoy short bursts of play, which mimics hunting or fighting behaviours.

By nature, cats are solitary predators but house cats can form close bonds with people, other cats and animals like dogs – especially if they have been socialized as kittens. To show affection, cats lick or cheek rub each other – or you. In fact, cats have scent glands on their cheeks, paws and flanks and rub against something to put their own personal scent on it. In addition, they use urine or poop to mark their territories or leave sexual messages for other cats.

If cats feel threatened by others, they will often fight to defend what they believe is their territory. Other ways cats communicate are through vocalizations – from purring and meowing to trilling, hissing, growling, snarling and grunting – and using body signals with their ears, tails, whiskers and eyes.

OPPOSITE:
Sleeping
Cats spend most of their time sleeping – on average, 15 hours a day, with kittens and older cats taking even longer snoozes. These are usually quick naps, or "catnaps", which allow cats to spring into action and do things like hunting prey.

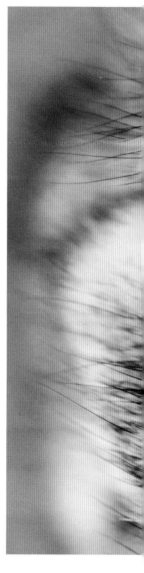

ABOVE:

Night vision

In the dark, cats can see six to eight times better than us, thanks to the many light receptors in their eyes called rods and a mirror-like structure in the back of the eye called the tapetum lucidum. The tapetum reflects any uncaught light that passes through the eye – this is what makes cats' eyes glow at night.

RIGHT:

Pupil shape

Viewed up close, a cat's eye has vertical slit pupils. Though it makes cats look terrifying, this allows them to see in bright daylight by limiting how much light enters their eyes. Conversely, in low light, the pupils expand – three times more than ours – to allow in additional light, and cover most of the eye.

PREVIOUS PAGES:
Cat vision

Cats are better adapted to seeing in low light – when they are usually more active – but they can also see colours. They can distinguish blues and yellows, whereas reds and greens can look grey or be confusing. Cat vision isn't as sharp as ours and so cats mostly rely on detecting movement.

RIGHT:
Whiskers

A cat's most prominent whiskers, or vibrissae, are on each side of the nose. These are loaded with nerves at their base and are highly sensitive. Whiskers help cats navigate in the dark or "see" up close by allowing them to locate objects through touch and air movements or vibrations. The deeply embedded whiskers are more than twice as thick as normal cat hairs.

ABOVE TOP:
Hunting

A young Maine coon shows off its whiskers. When hunting, whiskers help cats detect the exact location, shape and size of their prey – especially when it is too close to their mouth and they cannot see.

LEFT:
Super senses

With large eyes and ears and many whiskers, cats are adapted to be exceptional hunters – especially at dawn and dusk. Not only can they detect movement in low light, but they also have a powerful sense of smell and hearing.

OPPOSITE:
Touch

Except for the long whiskers on either side of the nose, cats have smaller whiskers on the cheeks, above the eyes and on the back of their front legs. Through touch and air currents, cats are able to create a 3D-like map of their surroundings that helps them navigate, whereby they can detect objects or obstacles, judge the width of gaps and even measure distances between objects.

LEFT TOP:
Unusual ears

Though most cats have upright ears, some are noted for having unusually shaped ears. Here, as a result of a genetic mutation, the Scottish fold has folded ears that bend forward and down towards the front of the head, giving the cat an "owl-like" look.

LEFT BOTTOM:
Ear tufts

Some cats have longer hairs on the tips of their ears, known as ear tufts. Quite what these hairs are for is unknown. It is possible that they work like whiskers and detect objects above the head or improve hearing. This Maine coon has both ear tufts and ear furnishings – hairs inside the ear.

OPPOSITE:
Hearing

Cats are able to detect high-pitched sounds, such as squeaking mice, that we cannot hear. The external part of their large ears, called pinnae, can be moved independently, which helps them amplify and locate the sound.

OPPOSITE TOP & BOTTOM:
Smell

A cat's nose is 14 times better than ours at picking up scents. Smell helps cats recognize people, objects, other cats or animals, as well as track their prey. Cats also use and leave smells for mating or to mark their territory and keep other cats away.

LEFT TOP:
Paw pads

Cat paws have a cushion-like pad under them to soften landings when they leap or jump off high places. These pads also help cats walk on rough ground and move and hunt quietly.

LEFT BOTTOM:
Natural cleaning

Cats start off cleaning themselves by licking their lips and paws. Their saliva contains a natural detergent-like substance that removes any scent and helps keep their fur clean.

LEFT:
Retractable claws

Cats normally have their curved claws hidden away, which helps keep them sharp. When they want to use them – to do anything from climbing to hunting, fighting and scratching to leave scent marks – cats flex the tendons in their paws.

OVERLEAF:
Tongue

A close-up of the cat's tongue shows the tiny hook-like spines called papillae. These are made of the protein keratin, just like human fingernails. Papillae act like a hair comb and allow large amounts of saliva to get to different layers of fur and right down to the skin for a deep clean. It also helps detangle their fur.

Bonded

Cats groom each other only when they already have a social bond. This activity is known as allogrooming, or social grooming, and is a sign of affection or bonding. Cats learn this behaviour from their mothers, meaning that a maternal instinct could likely play a role, too.

Grooming

Cats spend up to 50 per cent of their waking hours licking their coats. This keeps them clean and smooth, which helps protect their skin from infections. Cats always begin grooming themselves by licking their paws to use for cleaning their head and then work their way down the body.

Purr-fectly clean
A white fluffy, long-haired cat grooms its belly inside the house to keep its fur clean. It will lick, pull and bite at its fur to remove dead skin or hair, any detritus and parasites, and detangle it.

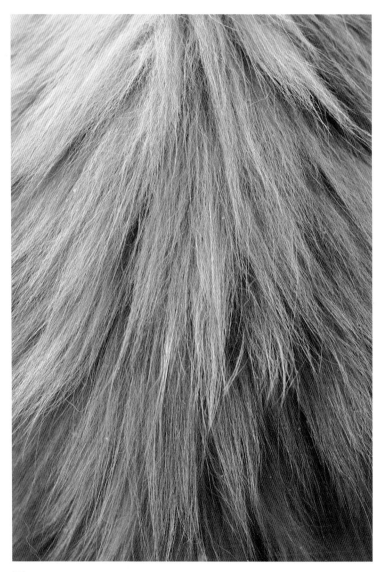

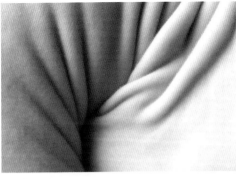

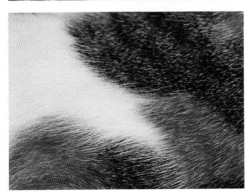

OPPOSITE:
Solid colour
Though most cats are shorthairs, some can have hair up to 12.5 cm (5 in) long. Coat colours that are only one colour and are without any patterns are known as "solid".

LEFT TOP:
Bare skin
Hairless cats, such as the sphynx or Donskoy, are not usually completely bald. Instead, they have a thin covering of fine fuzz. These cats end up having an oily skin and so need to be bathed on a regular basis.

LEFT MIDDLE:
Tabby
This coat pattern of stripes and swirls is called tabby. It can also have spots, blotches or whorls.

LEFT BOTTOM:
Calico
When a coat has multiple colours such as orange, black and white, the pattern is called calico. Although these three colours are the most common, some cats may have cream, red, chocolate brown or bluish-black.

ABOVE:
Balance
The vestibular apparatus in a cat's inner ear helps it monitor its balance while changing direction or speed. Even when falling, cats will reflexively twist their bodies and land on their paws.

LEFT:
Perching
Cats often like to sit in high places, or perch, so they can get a good view of their territory or hunt and strike their prey.

OPPOSITE:
Poised
A cat gets a better view while walking on a garden fence. Cats can get to high places because their powerful back legs allow them to jump six times their height.

171

PREVIOUS PAGES:
Friendship
Siblings show affection
by rubbing their heads
together. In addition to
doing this when they are
related, cats can become
friends with other cats if
they live together. When
cats share a home, they
create a group scent by
rubbing each other.

RIGHT:
Scent rubbing
A white cat head-rubs
against the leg of a table.
This leaves scents from
glands located on their
cheeks and marks the cat's
territory.

OPPOSITE TOP:
Hide and seek
Cats love small spaces and
often use bags or boxes as
hiding places. It is believed
that these provide comfort
and security, but they are
also good fun to play with!

OPPOSITE BOTTOM:
Unexpected friends
A cat and a dog play
together outdoors.
Though these two do
not naturally get along,
kittens socialized early on
are usually more friendly
and playful when meeting
other pets or animals.

Play

An adorable kitten plays with a furry toy mouse – its potential prey. As predators, cats imitate their hunting behaviour when playing. This allows kittens to practise hunting and learn to stalk, capture and kill prey.

Natural instincts
A kitten plays with a
dandelion outdoors.
Cats that are allowed
to go outside have more
opportunities to explore,
feed their curiosity and
follow their hunting
instincts.

Mating

Cats become sexually
mature between six and
nine months. Females
attract males, or tomcats,
by producing scents
and long wails known
as caterwauls. During
mating, the tomcat is on
top and bites the scruff of
the female's neck.

OPPOSITE TOP:
Loose skin

When cats are fighting,
their loose skin can help
them manoeuvre out of
a position and defend
themselves.

OPPOSITE BOTTOM:
Play fight

Cats will often roll
around, chase or
strike each other with
their paws, with claws
retracted. This so-called
play fighting is silent and
cats usually take turns.

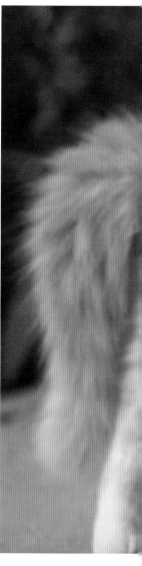

ABOVE TOP & BOTTOM:

Fighting

Cats are innately threatened by those from outside of their social group – especially males. When fighting, cats flatten their ears and hold them back to avoid damaging the inner parts, and puff up their fur on their backs or tails. Typically, fights do not last very long and the loser runs away with only a few scratches and bite marks.

RIGHT:

Fear

In the presence of a dog, this scared cat arches its back and raises its fur to appear bigger. When frightened, cats hold their ears to the sides and flatten their whiskers against their cheeks. In contrast, when threatened, cats hold their ears back and flat and their whiskers are forward.

LEFT ABOVE:
Ambush
Cats wait quietly, ready to pounce on their prey when it comes close enough to be captured.

LEFT BELOW:
Long-distance pouncers
Cats like the Maine coon are known for being adept hunters. They can accelerate quickly and pounce long distances to capture their prey.

OPPOSITE:
Stalking
Other cats hunt by actively stalking their prey and then run to catch it once they have sneaked up on it. Cats often like playing with their prey before killing it.

OPPOSITE:

Natural hunter

A crossbreed of the wild leopard cat and domestic shorthairs, the Bengal is a natural-born hunter. Here, a Bengal stalks its prey while sitting on a deck railing.

ABOVE:

Innate pouncer

This young spotted savannah, with huge ears and long legs, owes most of its looks and hunting abilities to the wild serval. Like its ancestor, it can suddenly spring on to its prey.

Kittens

Kittens are undeniably adorable at any age. When kittens are born – from spring to late autumn – they are completely helpless. Their eyes are sealed, their ears are folded and they are unable to keep themselves warm or feed on their own. This means kittens rely solely on their mothers for everything.

After a week or so, kittens start to open their baby blue eyes. Their true eye colour will not develop until the kitten is at least eight weeks old. From about two weeks of age until their seventh week, kittens grow very quickly – they become stronger and more co-ordinated, learn to groom themselves and others, and play games that instinctively include stalking, pouncing, jumping, biting, and clawing, which will later help them hunt. In fact, hunting behaviours appear to be hardwired into a cat's brain. At eight weeks, kittens will be more or less independent – and still remain cute.

Most cats have a litter of three to five kittens. However, some litters can reach up to ten kittens. Kittens will fully develop into their adult personality when they reach two years old. Regardless of breed, cats will generally be friendlier and able to get along with new people or other pets if they have been socialized from a young age.

OPPOSITE:
Abyssinian
This energetic, curious and intelligent breed, often seeking to play with its owners, is also known as the "clown of the cat kingdom".

Birman

With distinctive sapphire-blue eyes, white paws, a Roman nose and a long silky coat, this precious colourpoint kitten enjoys human company. The Birman was found in France in the 1920s but its exact origin is unknown. Legends say that the cats belonged to priests in ancient Myanmar, previously known as Burma or "*Birmanie*" in French – from where their name is derived.

OPPOSITE:
Exotic shorthair
This cuddly, gentle
kitten looks a lot like the
Persian with its rounded
head, flat face, full cheeks
and large, rounded eyes
– but with a shorter coat.
This is not surprising, as
the exotic shorthair is a
crossbreed of a Persian
and various short-haired
breeds, including the
American shorthair.

LEFT TOP:
Foldex
This tabby kitten with
somewhat folded ears,
also known as the exotic
fold, was developed in
Canada by crossing a
Scottish fold with an
exotic shorthair. Foldexes
get along with the whole
family and other pets and
are ideal for cuddles
and laps.

LEFT BOTTOM:
Highlander
With its distinctive curled
ears and a short tail,
this very playful and
attention-seeking kitten
makes a devoted and
lively companion in
any home.

193

American wirehair
This gentle, quiet and friendly wire-haired kitten is happy outdoors or indoors – though generally it prefers to stay indoors. It has a similar personality to its relative, the American shorthair.

American shorthair
With rounded faces, these adorable kittens are known for being affectionate to children, dogs and other pets. They can be found in more than 80 different colours and patterns.

American bobtail
These short-tailed – or "bobbed" -tailed – kittens are playful, sociable and generally love travelling and being among people. Native to the United States, American bobtails can have both a short and a long coat.

British shorthair
This adorable few-weeks'-old kitten doesn't like
too much attention. British shorthairs are quietly
affectionate and prefer to stay near their owners rather
than sitting on their laps or be picked up.

PREVIOUS PAGES:
Burmese
As they get older, these European Burmese kittens will not lose their energy, playfulness or cuteness, and will continue to enjoy themselves.

ABOVE:
Egyptian mau
This adorable kitten covered in spots is native to Egypt. Egyptian maus are playful, affectionate and loyal to their owners but generally do not take to strangers.

OPPOSITE:
Chartreux
These playful kittens that appear to be "smiling" take about two years to reach adulthood. Chartreux cats make great companions for all members of the family, including other animals.

Curly coat
Though Cornish rex cats have a curly or wavy coat, kittens can temporarily lose the curls for a few weeks. The curly coat is extremely fine and thus needs extra care.

OPPOSITE TOP:
Cornish rex
This playful, curious and energetic kitten remains the same as an adult and generally enjoys company – some even like to play fetch. Its big ears are thanks to the Siamese in its genes.

OPPOSITE MIDDLE:
Cyprus kittens
Native to Cyprus, this playful and affectionate cat are now being developed as a standardized breed under the name Aphrodite giant.

OPPOSITE BOTTOM:
Donskoy
This hairless kitten can sometimes have a partial fuzzy or wavy coat. In fact, some grow patches of fur in the winter. The Donskoy is friendly and active and is capable of learning commands.

RIGHT TOP:

Ragdoll

This precious kitten, nicknamed "dog-like cat", is affectionate, gentle and well-behaved and often follows people around. Ragdolls are also easy to handle and love sitting on laps.

RIGHT BOTTOM:

European shorthair

Developed from the domestic cats of Europe that were exceptional at hunting, this playful, friendly and intelligent European shorthair kitten will keep rodents away from both gardens and houses.

OPPOSITE:

Dragon li

This precious Chinese tabby kitten will become a large, muscular cat that will need space in which to keep active. In Chinese folklore, dragons are a symbol of power, strength and good luck.

ALL:
Devon rex

These unique-looking, mischievous kittens with short curly coats are nicknamed "pixie cats". Sometimes they appear to lack whiskers as these are short and often curly, too. The Devon rex is very active, playful and intelligent, and can learn tricks or be found jumping and exploring high places. Also affectionate, this cat loves to be perched on your shoulder or lap.

OPPOSITE TOP:
American curl
These curly-eared kittens
are born with straight
ears, which usually begin
to curl within a couple of
days and take their final
form at about the age of
four months. Their ears
must never be handled
because the cartilage
is firm and could be
damaged.

OPPOSITE BOTTOM:
Australian mist
Lively as a kitten,
the Australian mist is
affectionate and happily
lives indoors. It has
a spotted or marbled
coat with ticking that
resembles a mist. It is
very popular in Australia,
where it was developed in
the 1970s.

LEFT:
Arabian mau
This elegant young
Arabian mau with pointy
ears and often green,
slightly slanted oval eyes
was a desert dweller. It
can be found in many
colours and patterns,
including brown tabby.

Bengal
A mother licks her kitten to groom and show affection. Despite their wild-cat ancestry, Bengals are very affectionate to their owners, too.

OPPOSITE:
Oriental bicolour
This adorable kitten with almond-shaped eyes and bat-like ears comes with a strong personality. Active, playful and inquisitive, oriental bicolours can either be short haired or long haired.

ABOVE TOP:
Ojos azules
Thought to be active, affectionate and friendly, this beautiful blue-eyed kitten takes its name from the Spanish for "blue eyes".

ABOVE LOWER:
Mekong bobtail
Originally from South East Asia, this playful and affectionate kitten is noted for its bobbed tail, gorgeous blue eyes and colour-pointed coat, which is similar to that of a Siamese.

Himalayan
This litter of precious newborn kittens look like little fluffy balls of fur. Himalayans have long, thick coats that cover their entire bodies. They make great companions for humans because they are loving, calm and undemanding.

LaPerm

This kitten with very long curly whiskers looks like it has had a shaggy perm. Named for the coat, LaPerm cats are energetic, affectionate and enjoy human company.

Kanaani

With large ears and a long, spotted body, this lively kitten gets its looks and energy from its wild ancestor, the African wildcat.

OPPOSITE:

Modern Siamese

With a triangular-shaped head, large ears and blue almond-shaped eyes, this enchanting kitten is the most sociable and loud of all cats. Modern-style Siamese cats are intelligent, energetic and love lots of attention.

ABOVE:

Toyger

This feisty kitten resembles a tiny or "toy" tiger – a look that its breeder was going for. Toygers are intelligent, sociable and outgoing cats that enjoy playing games with their owners.

LEFT:

Snowshoe

With its distinctive white paws, this adorable kitten enjoys being around people or other pets and hates to be left on its own. Snowshoes are very clever and can open doors or play fetch.

OPPOSITE TOP:

Munchkin

This short-legged kitten is full of energy, runs quite fast and loves to play with the family. Munchkins can often have slightly longer back legs than front legs.

OPPOSITE BOTTOM:

Ukrainian levkoy

The unusual-eared kitten from Ukraine is playful, friendly and loves company – both from the family and other pets. Either hairless or with a very thin coat, Ukrainian levkoys have sensitive skin and need to be protected from the cold or direct sun.

LEFT:

Maine coon

This charming, fuzzy kitten with a bushy tail is the third most popular cat breed. Known as "gentle giants", Maine coons are intelligent and relaxed and often act like kittens their whole lives despite their huge size.

Russian blue
Energetic and curious,
Russian blues are great
climbers, leapers and
hunters but also quite shy
around unfamiliar faces.

BELOW:
Wichien maat
This highly intelligent
kitten is the original
Siamese. Wichien maats
are very energetic,
sociable and vocal
and will demand your
undivided attention.

Picture Credits

Alamy: 10 bottom (Imagebroker), 15 bottom (Jon G Fuller/VW Pics), 21 (Vince Burton), 22 top (Pardofelis Photography), 22 bottom (Anup Shah), 24 (Ernie James), 26 bottom (FGAM/cgwp.co.uk), 28 (Edo Schmidt), 32 bottom (Juniors Bildarchiv), 33 top (Xinhua), 34/35 (Pardofelis Photography), 42 (Tierfotoagentur), 44 bottom (Anny Lavrsen), 45 (Imagebroker), 48 bottom (Loop Images), 52 bottom (Dorling Kindersley), 62 right (Imagebroker), 63 (Serhii Kucer), 68 (Juniors Bildarchiv), 72 bottom (Tierfotoagentur), 75 (Bildagentur Geduligi), 81 (Dorling Kindersley), 106/107 (Planchard Eric/hemis.fr), 112 (Imagebroker), 117 bottom (Chris de Blank), 148 (Westend61), 166 bottom (David Bokuchava), 170 (Image Professionals), 171 top (Juniors Bildarchiv), 171 bottom (Martin Wilcox), 180 top (Imagebroker), 181 top (EyeEm), 184 (Arterra Picture Library), 185 bottom (Mauritius Images), 186 (Tripp Blunschi), 187 (Imagebroker), 194 (Juniors Bildarchiv), 203 top (Oleg Kozlov), 206 (Juniors Bildarchiv), 214/215 (Beautifulblossom), 216 (Tierfotoagentur), 217 (Juniors Bildarchiv)

Dreamstime: 6 (Guruxox),15 top (Slowmotiongli), 16 (Ondrej Prosicky), 38 (Martin Schneiter), 39 (Brett Critchley), 41 (Luca Santilli), 46 (Vladimir Akin'shin), 48 top (Noppadon Chanruangdecha), 50/51 (Ahmad Alfakharang), 57 (Atucknott), 61 bottom (Nicksu), 67 top right (Sergey Taran), 72 top (Anne Richard), 82/83 (Kalinin Dmitrii), 86 (Kucher Serhii), 88 top (Ivonne Wierink), 88 bottom (Dagmarhijmans), 95 (Clement Morin), 108 (Slowmotiongli), 114 bottom (Sergey Skleznev), 115 bottom (Paul-andre Belle-isle), 116 (Anna Krivitskaya), 117 top (Benophotography), 124/125 (Okoz77), 130 (Ian Mcglasham), 142 (Nelikz), 145 (Aleksandr Volchanskiy), 152/153 (Lucian Coman), 169 bottom (Tasakorn Kongmoon), 172/173 (Marco Clarizia), 181 bottom (Juha Jarrinen), 182 top (Davidtb), 182 bottom (Slowmotiongli), 205 (Li Cao), 213 bottom (Sergey Taran), 218 (Ivonne Wierink)

Shutterstock: 7 (Gita Kulinitch Studio), 8 (Jan Hejda), 10 top (Holly S Cannon), 11 (Holly Kuchera), 12 (Neil Lockhart), 13 top (Jack Bell Photography), 13 bottom (Ondrej Prosicky), 14 (Luis D Romero), 17 (Slowmotiongli), 18 (Ian Duffield), 19 (Stu Porter), 20 top, 20 bottom (Dennis W Donohue), 23 (Ondrej Prosicky), 25 (Sukpaiboonwat), 26 top (Vladimir Wrangel), 27 (Slowmotiongli), 30 top (Breaking The Walls), 30 bottom (Mukund Kumar), 31 (EcoPrint), 32 top (Eva Kohoutova), 33 bottom (Yiq), 36 (Matt Gibson), 37 top (Jim Cumming), 37 bottom (Michael Fitzsimmons), 40 (Anuradha Marwah), 44 top (Oksana Bystritskaya), 47 (Nitiphonphat), 49 (Fernando Calman), 52 top (JE Zygenjija), 53 (Daniel Thompson), 54/55 (Alexander Evgenyevich), 56 top (Seregraff), 56 middle (Oak Tree Studiostock), 56 bottom (Viktor Sergeevich), 58/59 (FotoMirta), 60 (Anastasiia Chystokoliana), 61 top (Galyna Andrushko), 62 top (Johanna Mehrke Fotografie), 64/65 (Yartseva), 66 top (Slowmotiongli), 66/67 bottom (Artsilence), 67 top left (Nynke Van Holten), 69 (Susan Leggett), 70 (Nikolai Tsvetkov), 71 top (Peefay), 71 bottom (Restimage), 73 (Atsupriatna24), 74 top (MDavidova), 74 bottom (SV-3t), 76 top (Alina Troeva), 76 bottom (Ires003), 77 (dien), 78 top (Kolomenskaya Kseniya), 78 bottom (Bingi Vamshi Krishna), 79 (Irina Nedikova), 80 (Bruno Passigatti), 84 (Bildagentuir Zoonar), 85 (Dizfoto), 87 (Suriya Nathan), 89 (nevodka), 90/91 (Jagodka) 92/93 (jojsmb), 94 top (Seregraff), 94 bottom (tkach-artvitae), 96/97 (Lus Kudritskaya), 98/99 (Slowmotiongli), 100 top (Anna Krivitskaya), 100 bottom (phichak), 101 (Kutikova Ekaterina), 102 (Seregraff), 104 top (nikkytok), 104 bottom (nadia-if), 105 (DragoNika), 109 top (Tine Robbe), 109 bottom (Borkin Vadim), 110/111 (Fazlyeva Kamilla), 113 (Dora Zett), 114 top (travelarium.ph), 115 top (Anne Richard), 118/119 (Oxana Oliferovskaya), 120/121 (samray), 122/123 (Dave's Domestic Cats), 126 top (Astrid Gast), 126 bottom & 127 (Elisa Putti), 128/129 (Anastasia Vetkovskaya), 131 top (Mariya Palagina), 131 bottom (Artem Kursin), 132/133 (Richard345), 134/135 (Eric Isselee), 136 (Nynke van Hotten), 137 (Serita Vossen), 138/139 (Vadim Petrakov), 140 (Nikolay Shargin), 141 (Sleptsova), 143 (Ciprian Gherghias), 144 top (Vasilisa Shtapakova), 144 bottom (Sundry Photography), 146/147 (Nedim Bajramovic), 150 (Maslowski Marcin), 151 (Nacho Mena), 154/155 (Nneirda), 156 (Valeri Potapova), 157 top (Nils Jacobi), 157 bottom (fantom_rd), 158 (schanz), 159 top (YuryKara), 159 bottom (Dennis Nata), 160 top (anueing), 160 bottom (Shvaygert Ekaterina), 161 top (Akmitova Tatiana), 161 bottom (G Ayala), 162/163 (Zarin Andrey), 164/165 (Nau Nau), 166 top (sophiecat), 167 (Luxurious Ragdoll), 168 (Zanna Pesnina), 169 top (Olgakan), 169 middle (mydegage), 174 (Sergey Skripko), 175 top (Pocket Canyon Photography), 175 bottom (vvvita), 176/177 (Nadinelle), 178/179 (Photo-SD), 180 bottom (Andrea Izzotti), 183 (fantom_rd), 185 top (SJ Duran), 188 (Parris Blue Productions), 190/191 (Daydream Photographic), 192 (andyyick), 193 top (Pherawit Rattanchot), 193 bottom (Susan Leggett), 195 top (Anurak Pongpatimet), 195 bottom (Ievgeniia Miroshnichenko), 196/197 (AnnaDonna), 198/199 (Seregraff), 200 (Artsilense), 201 (Tony Bowler), 202 (Kolomenskaya Kseniya), 203 middle (gka photo), 203 bottom (Kekyalyayness), 204 top (absolutimages), 204 bottom (helfei), 207 (OksanaSusoeva), 208 top (Seregraff), 208 bottom (OrangeGroup), 209 (SeraphP), 210/211 (PaPicasso), 212 (Kukurund), 213 top (Natalia Horiochykh), 219 top (Kutikova Ekaterina), 219 bottom (EVasilieva), 220 top (MDavidova), 220 bottom (Ravelios), 221 (Nils Jacobi), 222 top (Gita Kulinitch Studio), 222 bottom (Cup of Spring), 223 (Review News)